The Elon

Collection

Steve Gold

Table Of Contents

FREE BONUS NUMBER 1!

As a free bonus, I've included a preview of one of my other best-selling books, "Warren Buffett - The Business & Life Lessons Of An Investment Genius, Magnate & Philanthropist"! Go to the end of this book to read it.

ALSO...

Be sure to check out my other books. Go to the back of this book for a list of other books written by me, Steve Gold.

Book One Starts Here

Elon Musk

The Biography Of A Modern

Day Renaissance Man

Steve Gold

<u>Introduction</u>

When actor Robert Downey Jr. signed on to portray Tony Stark (a.k.a. Iron Man), he suggested to director John Favreau that they meet up with Elon Musk. They have a task of bringing to life a superhero, and Musk is the closest there ever is to Marvel's genius, billionaire, philanthropist in real life. The meeting was set and some of Musk's characteristics went into RDJ's portrayal of Tony Stark on screen, thus creating the memorable character that people come to know and love.

In reality, there is far more to Musk's life and person than can be personified by a fictional character. Sure, he does have a lot in common with Iron Man; he's a prodigious tech genius and entrepreneur, with the capacity to make seemingly impossible ideas a reality. Like Tony Stark, he dreams, thinks and lives large, but that is where the similarity ends.

Unlike his comic book counterpart, Elon Musk was not born into a life of luxury and ease. Despite showing potential for greatness as early as his preteens, his childhood and young adult life was filled with adversaries. To this day, Musk credits his early life struggles in helping him cultivate the indomitable spirit he is known for.

Having made his mark in the field of IT, finance, sustainable energy, automotive, aerospace manufacturing and space exploration, it is an understatement to say that Musk has come a long way from his humble beginnings. He founded some of the most pioneering companies – Paypal, Tesla Motors, and SpaceX – and is almost single-handed responsible for each enterprise's success. Whichever business he decided to dabble in, he brought with him a revolutionary idea which often ends up being a game-changer in the industry. Yet, he is far from done.

His brilliant mind never ceased to think up grander innovations, even after numerous repeated successful endeavors. His ample and wild ambitions, it seems, are driven by grand visions of changing the world we live in. His agenda for the future includes filling the roads with more electric cars, powering the world with solar energy, colonizing neighboring planets and enabling people to cover great distances with a futuristic high-speed public transportation system.

Most children would imagine of going outer space and travel to different cities in bullet-fast capsule pods, until those fantasies fade away in adulthood. Rarely are there individuals who dare to dream of living those fantasies that appropriately should stay within the realm of fiction. Elon Musk is among the exceptional few.

Table of contents

Chapter 1

The Beginnings Of Greatness

Almost every success story of high-achieving individuals contain episodes highlighting their extraordinary iron will, critical thinking, propensity for hard work, and an unwavering belief that the impossible is not out of their reach. As one of the most brilliant minds who help shaped the global economy after at the dawn of the information age and tech boom in the late 20th century, it is hardly surprising that Elon Musk displayed such distinctive personality traits at an incredibly young age.

Elon Reeve Musk was born in June 28 of 1971, in Pretoria, Gauteng, South Africa. His father is a South African-born British electrical engineer, Errol Musk, and his mother is Canadian-English dietitian, Maye Musk. Elon is the eldest of their three children, followed by brother Kimbal and sister Tosca.

Growing up in Pretoria, Elon's early years were far from a picture perfect childhood. His parents divorced when he was 9 years-old, after which he lived mostly with his demanding and emotionally abusive father. At school, he endured harsh bullying by his peers. In one notable instance, he ended up hospitalized after being pushed down a flight of stairs. Such ordeals led Elon to find solace in the safest company available; his own thoughts and imagination which resided in the deep recesses of his prodigious mind.

He would regularly immerse himself in reading as a means of escaping his troubles in the outside world. Encyclopedias and science fiction were among his favorite books; they added to his knowledge bank and encouraged his seemingly wild dreams of futuristic technology which had yet to become a reality. Often times, Elon would be caught daydreaming and lost in his own thoughts, ignoring the world around him in favor of the utopias in his imagination. Along with his innovative thoughts, Elon's childhood experiences also contributed to him developing a high tolerance for hardship and an extraordinary work ethic; attributes which he is well known for and which have served him well in his life.

His aptitude for technological innovations and entrepreneurship was evident when he began teaching himself computer programming at the tender age of 10. When he was just 12, he developed a spaceship shooter video game called, "Blastar", which he sold to a computer magazine for $500. After his first brush with success, Elon and his younger brother, Kimbal, hatched a plan to open an arcade near their school. Unfortunately, their enterprising plan had to be scrapped when their parents refused to provide the legal consent to obtain a business permit.

In 1988, after graduating from Pretoria Boys High School at the age of 17, Elon made the momentous decision to leave his hometown for the United States, without the support of his parents. This would be the first step towards his hard-earned success. He was able to obtain Canadian citizenship through his mother a year later, and left South Africa for

Montreal, Canada. There, he worked low-paying jobs and was living on the brink of poverty for a year.

At the age of 19, he was accepted into Queens University in Kingston, Ontario for undergraduate studies in science. It was during his studies that he met Canadian author, Justine Musk, whom he would marry in 2000 and end up having six sons with. Their marriage lasted for only eight years, and Elon got married for the second time to British actress Talulah Riley. This marriage ended in divorce in 2014.

Two years into his studies at Queens, Elon received a scholarship from The University of Pennsylvania (Penn) in America. He relocated to the US in 1992, following his transfer to Penn. In the following year, he earned his Bachelor of Science degree in Physics from Penn's College of Arts and Sciences, and stayed back a year at Penn's Wharton School to complete his studies for a Bachelor of Science degree in Economics.

Throughout his college years, alongside his scientific studies, Elon took a keen interest in philosophical and religious literature. It was stated that his all-time favorite book is *The Hitchhiker's Guide to the Galaxy* by Douglas Adams. It is through this immersion in both science and personal studies of humanities that Elon found his calling; he had the lofty ambition of wanting to contribute to projects that would change the world for the better.

Consequently, his vision and entrepreneurial aspirations began taking shape, specifically in the areas of the internet, renewable energy and space exploration.

Chapter 2

Young Promise Fulfilled

Having earned his academic credentials and being in the right environment where his brilliance was highly appreciated, the 24 year-old Elon would soon make a significant decision which changed his life, and ended up revolutionizing the way business is conducted over the internet. Elon enrolled in a Ph.D. program in the field of applied physics and material science with the graduate school at Stanford University.

It was the summer of 1995, the dot-com boom was still in its early stages. Despite the rapid development and growth of the internet, no one had yet to make a vast fortune from this vehicle which would eventually become a ubiquitous part of life for a vast number of people around the globe. After just two days of class, Elon dropped out of his doctorate program to heed the call of his enterprising spirit.

With $28,000 of their father's (Errol Musk) money, brothers Elon and Kimbal started a software company called, Zip2. The company developed and marketed a sort of online city guide for the newspaper publishing industry, providing a platform where newspaper publishers could offer additional content and services to their customer. Zip2 boasted a few highly impressive contractors, including but not limited to *The New York Times* and *Chicago Tribune*.

The first two years in business wasn't easy for Elon and he struggled with his first company. He worked diligently for 10 to 12 hours daily, plodding away from early morning until late evening. He lived very minimally during this period; his rented office doubled as a home, and he would take showers at the locker rooms of a nearby local stadium. The accumulated money he saved from living in such a frugal manner was used to keep the company afloat. In a struggle to keep his business alive, Elon eventually sold a majority of Zip2 shares to venture capitalists in exchange for $3.6 million in investment.

His perseverance would pay off in 1999 when the biggest search engine of that time, AltaVista – which was later acquired by Compaq Computer Corporation – bought Zip2 for $307 million in cash and $34 million in securities. The amount was a record-breaking deal and out of the total sum, Elon's own share was $22 million. The acquisition practically made him an overnight millionaire at the age of 28. To celebrate his success, he bought himself a new condominium, a McLaren F1 and a 12-seat Dassault 900 private jet.

Having made himself considerable a fortune at a relatively young age, Elon could have taken time off to bask in his achievements and enjoy his newly acquired wealth. However, the prodigal tech wizard was just getting started after his first monumental success.

Ready to aim higher and build greater innovations for mankind, Elon started his next company that same year, a very short time after selling Zip2.

Chapter 3

From X.com to PayPal

Making the foray into the area of personal finance was anything but smooth-sailing for Elon. For starters, he lacked experience in this complex field. The investors he sought found the idea of a full-service online banking system too risky, if not downright undoable.

Not one to back away in the face of adversary, Elon stood by his vision of a new and improved financial service that utilized the connectivity of the internet. He went on ahead and started the online banking company, X.com, with $10 million dollars from the sale of Zip2 in 1999. He then invented the method of securely transferring money online using only a recipient's e-mail address.

A year later, X.com merged with Confinity, a rival company ran by Max Levchin and Peter Thiel. Confinity was a company specializing in developing security software for handheld devices, with one of their creations being the world's first digital wallet, Paypal. Optimistic that the money transfer service would be an enormous success, Elon directed his focus on developing Paypal into a global payment transfer provider. His optimism, however, wasn't shared by then-president, Bill Harris who disagreed on some fundamental aspects of the plan.

Elon stood by his vision and once again, his determination paid off; Harris left the company in May 2000. In October of that same year, Elon decided to terminate the online banking operations he had developed before the merger, and make PayPal the company's flagship service. The company was renamed PayPal in 2001.

Elon's new direction for the company did incur some disagreements with his new team when it came to strategy and management, but the internal conflict did not affect the company's growth. Musk developed a new business model and a viral marketing campaign. His strategy was an immense success as the number of customers who signed up for the service increased rapidly throughout the year, as did the company's revenues.

The company went public in the following year at $13 per share, and generated over $61 million. PayPal would go on to become a highly trusted company in the field and the PayPal is now synonymous with internet monetary services.

Later in 2002, eBay bought PayPal for $1.5 billion. As the biggest shareholder at the time, Elon received $180 million for his share from the sale, and an additional $165 million in stock from the online auctions giant as part of the deal.

With repeated success over the short span of 4 years, most people assumed that Elon would simply retire from the limelight and settle on becoming a venture capitalist. But early retirement was never appealing for Elon despite the fact he had already made his mark in the field of integrated technology. He was now ready to expand his world-changing vision by making a foray into space exploration and energy resources.

Chapter 4

Tesla Motors

Leaving the internet industry behind, Elon co-founded what would be the first of his three biggest ventures – the electric vehicle manufacturer, Tesla Motors. The company was actually founded a year before Elon came into the project, by engineers Martin Eberhard and Marc Tarpenning. It was founded on the dream of freeing vehicle users from the oil burden, and was positioned as the first serial manufacturer of electric vehicles. Elon loved the aspiration, finding it rather inline with his own.

In 2004, Elon entered the project as chairman of the board of directors, with a personal investment of $7.5 million, a sum which made him the controlling investor. At first, he did not partake in the operational management of the company, and only handled the production side of the business. He participated in designing one of their first electric cars, the Tesla Roadster, which was in-part based on the British Lotus Elise.

Elon was meticulous in his designing of the Tesla Roadster. He was adamant that carbon fiber composite materials be used in the hull to minimize weight. He also developed and refined the battery module, and even had a hand in the aesthetic design elements. Under his supervision, the project garnered media attention by 2006, and Elon was awarded the

Global Green 2006 product design award for the design of the Tesla Roadster. With the exposure it received, Tesla Motors continued to grow, attracting big investors including the creators of Google, Larry Page and Sergey Brin, former eBay President Jeff Skoll, and Hyatt heir Nick Pritzker. During this period, the company accumulated over $100 million in investment.

By 2007, the Tesla Roadster was ready to enter the production phase, and was released to the public soon after. Things were looking promising until the company encountered its first of several hurdles. Failures in production management led to the actual selling price of the car being almost double the originally intended price of $92,000. Additionally, Martin Eberhard made a miscalculation that meant his concept of transmission for the Tesla Roadster was to be ineffective. There was no choice but to postpone the release of the electric vehicle for more than a year.

In times of crisis, Elon remained resilient, thanks in part to his arduous childhood and young adult life. He immediately took it upon himself to restructure the company. First, he terminated everyone who had stalled the Tesla Roadster project's development; including Eberhard and a few other key players. After the cleanup, he took over the management of the company himself. The position of CEO was assumed by Michael Marks after the departure of Eberhard. Marks was then succeeded by Ze'ev Drori in December 2007, before Elon himself took over as CEO with Drori becoming Vice Chairman in December 2008.

In a vigorous effort to further cut costs, Elon downsized the workforce, demanded lower prices from suppliers, and closed some of the offices. As a result, the Tesla Roadster was finally unveiled to the world in February of 2008 with a minor – less than $20,000 – increase in the originally intended price.

The streak of bad luck was far from over for Elon, though. In late spring of 2008, he filed for divorce from his wife Justine, for reasons undisclosed to the public. Later, that same October, Tesla Motors faced another financial crisis. The company was on the verge of bankruptcy, and Elon was determined not to let all his hard work go down the pipes. After all, the company was built on his own personal vision of a world less depended on oil.

Elon believed that oil dependency leads to climate change and geopolitical tensions, and that making the switch from internal combustion engines to electric motors could make a huge difference for humanity on a global scale.

In order to save Tesla Motors, he decided to put all his eggs in this one basket. He poured in additional funds received from taking over a software development company, Everdream, where he was the main shareholder. To retain the trust of customers and to prevent them from bailing out, Elon gave personal guarantees that they would receive a refund in the event of the business failing. He even sold his beloved McLaren F1 and invested the last $20 million of his personal fortune into the company.

Not only did Elon manage to save Tesla Motors from bankruptcy, he managed to turn the company's fortunes around. German multinational automotive corporation, Daimler, took an interest in Tesla Motors, and made an investment of $50 million to help save it. Recognizing the potential, the UD Department of Energy authorized decided that Tesla Motors should be included in a pool of innovative transport companies and granted it a preferential interest-bearing loan.

On June 29, 2010, Tesla Motors became the second car manufacturer in the US – after Ford in 1956 – to enter the Initial Public Offering (IPO) market. Despite being unprofitable for almost a decade, the company was listed on the NASDAQ at $17 per stock and attracted more than $225 million of investment. The market entry could not have been more perfectly timed as the oil slick that covered a significant part of the Gulf of Mexico, due to the fault of British Petroleum, was growing. The incident raised the issue of making the transition to alternative fuels, and this now seemed evermore favorable.

In 2012, the company started the production of the Tesla Model S, an electronic Sedan with a battery that supplies 265 miles (426 km) of range. At the unveiling of the Model S, Elon confidently stated that in 20 years, more than half of all vehicles produced would be electric. His forecast, of course, was dismissed by most analysts. Even so, critics would be the last people to faze the visionary CEO of Tesla Motor, because to Elon, as long as he can dream it, he can create it.

The Model S was a success, selling 10,500 units during the first half of 2013, shortly after being made available to the public. In addition to being environmentally friendly, the electric vehicle touted a number of innovative state-of-the-art features that were previously only dreamt of or seen in the likes of science fiction movies, such as automatic lane change, the ability to indicate and avoid pedestrians and collisions, and even the ability to read speed limit signs. It was hardly a surprise the the Model S was rated by Consumer Report as the best car in the world for two years in a row, in 2013 and 2014.

Under Elon's leadership, Tesla Motors' technology is not only revolutionizing the automotive industry, but could also be changing the way the world uses energy. Tesla Motors' engineers have cooperated with other car manufacturers, such as Daimler and Toyota to create more energy-efficient 'hybrid' cars – vehicles equipped with an electric motor and an internal combustion engine. The company also built a network of hundreds of Supercharger stations across North America. These stations are to electric cars what gasoline stations are to the ordinary vehicle. There are currently over 2,300 Superchargers in the world, across North America, Europe and Asia.

On May 01, 2015, Tesla Motors introduced a wall mounted, rechargeable lithium ion battery with liquid thermal control for home use, called the Powerwall. The battery is intended to store electricity for domestic consumption, load shifting, and backup power. Tesla Motors also introduced a solution for heavy energy consumption, called the Powerpack. It can be used in offices, industrial facilities, and utilities.

According to Elon, 160 million Powerpack units would be enough to provide energy to all consumers in the United States, while 2 billion units would be enough to power the whole world.

Chapter 5

Space X - Otherworldly Ambitions!

Like most children who grew up with science fiction novels, Elon was fascinated with the idea of exploring outer space and reaching other planets in the solar system. He had ambitions of colonizing Mars by creating an oasis and establishing a greenhouse on the red planet. It was the kind of childhood fantasy that most kids eventually grow out of, but that was not the case for Elon though, as he was set on making those ideas a reality.

He was already a long-standing member of the Mars Society, a nonprofit organization that supports the exploration of Mars. In 2002, he started Space Exploration Technologies, or SpaceX, for short. Headquartered in Hawthorne, California, USA, the private aerospace manufacturer was set up to develop the rocket technology that he hoped would someday accommodate his ambitious idea. For this project, he envisioned a cost-effective means of space transportation that would enable humanity to colonize Mars. His goal for the project were to create automated greenhouses on the surface of a neighboring planet, which in the future could serve as a basis for a self-sustaining ecosystem. As ridiculously ambitious as the goal was, Elon invested more than $100 million in SpaceX on March 2006.

There was one big problem standing in the way of this grand aspiration; the cost of delivering greenhouses to Mars was simply too humongous for the entrepreneur to bear. Still, never knowing when to give up, Elon was ready to try any means possible, including ordering launch vehicles from the Russian Federation. After some discussion with Russian officials, an agreement could not be reached and a deal between the parties could not be agreed. Elon attributed the high cost of launch vehicles to the low levels of competition among large corporations within the space industry. He then came up with the idea of designing his own reusable launch vehicles and spaceships.

Elon was convinced that the costs of creating and launching launch vehicles and spaceships could be reduced tenfold. First, he needed to redefine the goal of the spaceflight mission that SpaceX was looking to carry out. The aim was not the delivery of astronauts and cargo into orbit, but the colonization of nearby planets as efficiently as possible.

In 2008, Founders Fund, a venture capital firm that belonged to Elon's former PayPal partners, Peter Thiel and Dave McClure, became the first supporter of SpaceX. A year later, another venture capital firm, DFJ Ventures, pitched in and in 2010, both firms led another round of investments that enabled SpaceX to raise $50.2 million.

In truth, SpaceX had started working on the Falcon 1 launch system way back in 2002. The project was headed by renowned rocket engineer Tom Mueller, and named after the Millennium Falcon spaceship of the Star Wars movies. The rocket took four years and hundreds of millions of dollars in private funding to design. In the period of 2006 through 2015, several companies had taken interest in SpaceX's project, including DARPA, NASA, ORS, Celestis, ATSB, SpaceDev, Orbcomm, NSPO and Astrium.

SpaceX conducted three test launches of the Falcon 1 from 2006 to 2008, all of which failed. With the patience of investors wearing thin, the very fate of SpaceX lay in the fourth launch attempt. The fourth time proved to be a charm for SpaceX as Falcon 1 finally reached orbit on 28 September 2008. Impressed by the achievement, NASA signed a contract with SpaceX for 12 delivery flights to and from Earth orbit using the SpaceX robotic Dragon spacecraft and their Falcon 9 rocket. Following its first success, SpaceX went on to develop several types of rocket engines, such as the Kestrel, Merlin 1, Draco and Super Draco without any support from the government, and relying solely on public funding. Some of the company's projects are meant as innovations in aerospace manufacturing, designed with the intention of transporting people from Earth to Mars in the future.

From a business standpoint, it seemed to make sense for SpaceX to enter the IPO market. However, Elon has other priorities for his space exploration company; to him, SpaceX is a means to achieving his biggest dream of conducting an expedition to Mars. In fact, he once boldly said that he would like to die on the surface of Mars, but not just from the landing impact.

On February 12, 2015, SpaceX reached another milestone achievement when the Falcon 9 rocket successfully delivered the Deep Space Climate Observatory (DSCOVR) satellite to orbit from SpaceX's Launch Complex 40 located at Cape Canaveral Air Force Station. Developed in collaboration with NOAA, NASA and the United States Air Force, the satellite was launched to detect and inform of any extreme emissions from the sun, which could affect communications infrastructures, other satellites close to the Earth and power grids.

Elon reported the success of the launch and vertical landing of the rocket through Twitter, optimistically and somewhat idealistically, stating that what was previously imagined in science fiction can become a reality in a decade or two.

Chapter 6

SolarCity

Elon's vision of creating a world with affordable and accessible clean energy did not end with the success of Tesla Motors. In 2003, he sold 11% of his PayPal stocks to invest $10 million in SolarCity Corporation, a photovoltaics products and services company founded by his cousins Lyndon and Peter Rive.

SolarCity provides solar power systems for homes, businesses and governments. Among their initiatives to make solar power available to homeowners are programs such as the MyPower loan and the Solar Power Purchase Agreement (PPA). Not only is the company's concept cost effective and environmentally sound, they are completely in line with Elon's own principles. Hence, SolarCity became the solar energy systems provider for Tesla Motors' Supercharger stations.

Despite most industry leaders knowing what Elon is capable of as an innovator in the field, some critics were still skeptical that solar electric power could ever truly be turned into a viable and effective business model. Their skepticism was based on the fact that competition is too high in the industry, and it would be too great of a challenge for a company to stay in the leading position. The market begs to differ, though.

Since SolarCity entered the IPO market in 2012, its stock value went from $8 to $11.79. The company's share stock price continues to rise, and as of February 13, 2015, the share stock price was $57.60, with the total market capital at $5.53 billion.

Amazed by this phenomenon, analytics attributed Elon's involvement and assurance in the company's prospects to be the main reason for its success. The Wall Street society named this phenomenon *The Musk Effect*. Somehow, the public perceives that if the creator of SpaceX and Tesla Motors is vouching for a certain technology, then it means that there must truly be something to it.

Chapter 7

Hyperloop

Whether it be internet services, space exploration or clean energy, Elon managed to accomplish what most people would dismiss as impossible. He is an innovator driven by boundless ambitions to change the world. It seems like his imagination never stops conjuring bigger and better ideas. What more can one do to ensure a future that relies on clean, sustainable solar energy? If it is up to Elon, he would like to revolutionize mass transit.

On August 12, 2013, he published a blog post explaining his concept for a mode of transportation called Hyperloop – an idea he thought out during his spare time. More than just shedding light on its structure and function, Elon published a comprehensive presentation which included sketches, charts, maps and specific technical information.

Hyperloop is a solar-powered, high-speed transportation system which can theoretically enable people to travel from Los Angeles to San Francisco – covering the distance of 381.8 miles (614.44 km) – in a mere 30 minutes. The concept is based on the technology of magnetic levitation (mag-lev) trains. Basically, people would be transported inside aluminum pods enclosed inside of steel tubes, mounted on columns 50 to 100 yards apart, with these tubes being able to travel up to a staggering 800 miles per hour.

One pod would be able to accommodate up to 28 people, and if the budget of the project were sufficient, the Hyperloop cargo pods would also be able to hold and transport up to three cars in each.

Elon even thought of the operating details of the Hyperloop; there would be 70 capsules on the preliminary route with a minimum delay interval of 30 seconds. This is to accommodate the 5 miles safe distance between the capsules. A one-way ticket to ride the Hyperloop would be priced at an extremely reasonable $20, and with the system transporting at least 7.4 million passengers each way, it would take 20 years to see a payback on investment. Not to mention, people would no longer have to endure the currently available, relatively slow methods of transportation, when commuting to large cities located at a distance of not more than 900 miles from each other.

Elon believes that Hyperloop could be a less costly alternative to the US government's plan of spending more than $70 billion on a high-speed railroad between San Francisco and Los Angeles. His other companies could pitch in the resources for making Hyperloop a reality; the motors and electronics of the capsules could be derived from Tesla Motors, engineers from SolarCity could work on the solar panels that would power the system, and SpaceX could provide the sturdy materials that have been tested for durability in space.

Taking into account safety measures in the engineering, Elon ensured that the design will include unprecedented levels of safety for passengers when talking about the concept to the media. Hyperloop will have an emergency braking system, and even elements for leveling the risk of destruction in case of an earthquake.

Not ready to devote the required time to the concept himself, Elon decided to make the Hyperloop design an open source, allowing everyone to improve the current version of it. On February 26, 2015, the research company that was formed using crowd sourcing and collaboration, Hyperloop Transportation Technologies (HTT), received the green light to build the first full-scale test track. Construction is set to begin in 2016, at the California model town of Quay Valley, and to be completed by 2019.

If it is built, Hyperloop will be a mode of transportation faster than any means of travel that has ever existed; twice as fast as a plane. In addition, it will not be limited to any schedule. Perhaps the futuristic utopia that had only existed in the realm of imagination is closer to becoming a reality than we realize, all thanks to the big vision of the brilliant industrialist, inventor and modern day renaissance man, Elon Musk.

Chapter 8

Elon's Caltech Commencement Address

Friday, June 15, 2012

I was trying to think what's the most useful thing that I can say to be useful to you in the future. And I thought, perhaps tell the story of how I sort of came to be here. How did these things happen? Maybe there are lessons there. I often find myself wondering, how did this happen.

When I was young, I didn't really know what I was going to do when I got older. People kept asking me. Eventually, I thought the idea of inventing things would be really cool. The reason I thought that was because I read a quote from Arthur C. Clark, 'A sufficiently advanced technology is indistinguishable from magic.' That's really true. If you go back say, 300 years, the things we take for granted today, you'd be burned at stake for. Being able to fly. That's crazy. Being able to see over long distance, being able to communicate, the Internet as a group mind of sorts, and having access to all the word's information instantly from anywhere on the earth. This really would be considered magic in times past.

In fact, I think it goes beyond that, there's many things we take for granted today that weren't even imagined in times past, so it goes beyond that. So I thought, If I can do some of those things -- if I can advance technology, that is like magic and that would be really cool.

I always had an existential crisis, trying to figure out 'what does it all mean?' I came to the conclusion that if we can advance the knowledge of the world, if we can expand the scope and scale of consciousness, then, we're better able to ask the right questions and become more enlightened. That's the only way to move forward.

So, I studied physics and business, because in order to do these things you need to know how the universe works and how the economy works and you also need to be able to bring people together to create something. It's very difficult to create something as individuals if it's a significant technology.

So, I came out to California to figure out how to improve the density of electric vehicles, if there's an advanced capacitor, to serve as an alternative to batteries. That was in 1995. That's when the Internet started to happen. I thought I could either pursue this technology, where success may not be one of the possible outcomes, which is always tricky, or participate in the Internet and be part of it. So, I decided to drop out. Fortunately, we're past graduation, so, cannot be accused of recommending that to you. [Laughter]. I did some Internet stuff, [Laughter] you know. I've done a few things here and there. One of which is PayPal.

Maybe it's helpful to say, one of the things important in the creation of PayPal was how it started. Initially, the goal with PayPal was create a conglomeration for financial services, so all financial services could be seamlessly integrated to work smoothly. And we had a little feature, e-mail payments. Whenever we'd show the system off, we'd show the hard part, the conglomeration of financial services, which is difficult to put together. Nobody was interested. Then we showed people e-mail payments, which was easy to put together, and everyone was interested. So, it's important to take feedback from your environment. You want to be as closed-loop as possible.

So, we focused on e-mail payments and tried to make that work. That's when really good things started to take off. But, if we hadn't responded to what people said, we probably would not have been successful. So, it's important to look for things like that and focus on that, and correct your prior assumptions.

Going from PayPal, I thought well, what are some of the other problems that are likely to most affect the future of humanity? Not from the perspective, 'what's the best way to make money,' which is okay, but, it was really 'what do I think is going to most affect the future of humanity.' The biggest terrestrial problem is sustainable energy. Production and consumption of energy in a sustainable manner. If we don't solve that in this century, we're in deep trouble. And the other thing I thought might affect humanity is the idea of making life multi-planetary.

The latter is the basis for SpaceX and the former is the basis for Tesla and SolarCity. When I started SpaceX, initially, I thought that well, there's no way one could start a rocket company. I wasn't that crazy. But, then, I thought, well, what is a way to increase NASA's budget? That was actually my initial goal. If we could do a low cost mission to Mars, Oasis, which would land with seeds in dehydrated nutrient gel, then hydrate them upon landing. We'd have a great photo of green plants with a red background [Laughter]. The public tends to respond to precedence and superlatives. This would be the first life on Mars and the furthest life had ever traveled.

That would get people excited and increase NASA's budget. But the financial outcome would be zero. Anything better would on the upside. So, I went to Russia three times to look at buying a refurbished ICBM... [Laughter] ...because that was the best deal. [Laughter] And I can tell you it was very weird going late 2001-2002 to Russia and saying 'I want to buy two of your biggest rockets, but you can keep the nukes.' [Laughter] The nukes are a lot more. That was 10 years ago.

They thought I was crazy, but, I did have money. [Laughter] So, that was okay. [Laughter] After making several trips to Russia, I came to the conclusion that, my initial impression was wrong about not enough will to explore and expand beyond earth and have a Mars base. That was wrong. There's plenty of will, particularly in the United States. Because United States is the nation of explorers, people came here from other parts of the world. The United States is a distillation of the spirit of human exploration. If people think it's impossible and it's going to break the budget, they're not going to do it.

So, after my third trip, I said, okay, what we need to do already is try to solve the space transport problem and started SpaceX. This was against the advice of pretty much everyone I talked to. [Laughter]. One friend made me watch videos of rockets blowing up.

[Laughter] He wasn't far wrong. It was tough going there in the beginning. I never built anything physical. I never had a company that built something physical. So, I had to bring together the right team of people. We did all that, then, failed three times. It was tough, tough going.

Think about a rocket, the passing grade is 100%. And you don't get to test the real environment that the rocket is going to be in. So, I think the best analogy for rocket engineers, if you want to create complicated software, you can't run as an integrate whole, or run on the computer it's intended to run on, but, first time you run it, it has to run with no bugs. That's the essence of it. So, we missed the mark there.

The first launch, I was picking up bits of rocket at the launch site. And we learned with each successive flight. And were able to, eventually in 2008, reach orbit. Also that was with the last bit of money we had. Thank goodness that happened. Fourth time is the charm? [Laughter].

So, we got the Falcon 1 to orbit. Then, began to scale it up to Falcon 9, with an order of magnitude more thrust, around a million pounds of thrust. We managed to get that to orbit, then developed the Dragon spacecraft, which recently docked to the space station and returned to earth.

[Applause] That was a white knuckle event. [Laughter]. It was a huge relief. I still can't believe it actually happened. Yet, there's more to happen for humanity to become a multi-planet species. It's vitally important. And I hope that some you have will participate in that at SpaceX or other companies. It's really one of the most important things for the preservation and extension of consciousness. It's worth noting that Earth has been around for 4 billion years, but civilization in terms of having writing is only about 10,000 years, and that's being generous.

So, it's really somewhat of a tenuous existence that civilization and consciousness has been on earth. I'm actually fairly optimistic about the future earth. I don't want to give the wrong impression like we're all about to die. [Laughter] I think things will be okay for a long time on earth. Not for sure, but, most likely. But even if it's 99% likely, a 1% chance is still worth the effort to back up the biosphere, and achieved planetary redundancy. [Laughter]. And I think it's really quite important.

And in order to do that, there's great things that is need to occur. Create a rapidly reusable transport system to Mars. It's something right on the borderline of impossible. But, that's the sort of the thing that we're going to try to achieve with SpaceX.

And then, on the Tesla front, the goal was to show what electric cars can do. We had to change people's perceptions. They used to think electric cars were slow and ugly, with low range, like a golf cart. So, we created Tesla Roadster, a vehicle to show that it's fast, attractive and long range. Even though you can show something on paper, and the calculations are clear, until you have physical object, it doesn't really sink in.

If you're going to create a company, you need to create a working prototype. Everything works great on PowerPoint. You can make anything work on

PowerPoint. If you have a demonstration model, even in primitive form, that's much more effective in convincing people. So we made the Roadster, and now we're coming out with model S, a 4-door sedan. Some people said, 'sure you can make an expensive small volume car, but can you make a real car?' Okay, fine, we're going to make that, too. [Laughter] So, that's coming out.

And so that's where things are and hopefully, there are lessons to be drawn there.

I think the overreaching point I want to make is you guys are the magicians of the 21th century, don't let anything hold you back. Imagination is the limit. Go out there and create some magic.

Thank you.

(Note: Please be aware that this transcript may not be

strictly verbatim.)

Conclusion

Elon Musk's abilities seem unlimited and he is unquestionably a supremely driven individual who has already achieved some truly outstanding feats. Not only that, but he is still a relatively young man and with his seemingly insatiable drive and ambition it seems almost inevitable that he will achieve much more during the remainder of his life.

From relatively humble beginnings to making the seemingly unachievable a reality, Elon Musk's story so far illustrates how much one man can do if they put their mind to it. I for one am looking forward to seeing what is in store from Elon Musk from this point forward.

Check Out My Other Books!

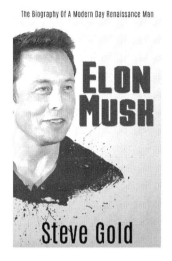

Elon Musk - The Biography Of A Modern Day

**Renaissance ManElon Musk - The Business &
Life Lessons Of A Modern Day Renaissance
Man**

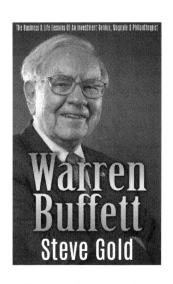

Warren Buffett - The Business And Life Lessons Of An Investment Genius, Magnate And Philanthropist

Steve Jobs - The Biography & Lessons Of The Mastermind Behind Apple

Management - Achieve Management Excellence & World Class Leadership Skills In 7 Simple Steps

Sales - Easily Sell Anything To Anyone & Achieve Sales Excellence In 7 Simple Steps

Arduino - Getting Started With Arduino: The Ultimate Beginner's Guide

(If the links do not work, for whatever reason, you can simply search for these titles on the Amazon to find them. All books available as ebooks or printed books)

Book Two Starts Here

Elon Musk

The Business & Life Lessons

Of A Modern Day

Renaissance Man

Steve Gold

<u>Introduction</u>

Enduring entrepreneurial success – especially in repeated bouts of hugely profitable ventures – is never a product of chance. It is a result of patience, hard work and unwavering perseverance in the face of adversity. In addition to these qualities, one needs to be guided by a clear world-changing vision to serve humanity that surpasses oneself. All these qualities – among others – have lead to Elon Musk's monumental success in the various endeavors he had chosen to pursue.

Growing up in a dysfunctional household, Musk had his first encounter with success at the age of 12 when he sold the program for a video game of his creation for $500. His prodigious tech wizardry and propensity for entrepreneurship never stopped growing, leading him to build upon each venture, with each successive achievement being a little bigger than the one before.

He changed the game in the financial sector when he revolutionized monetary services online with the founding of Paypal, despite knowing very little about financial services at the time, all the while having to face the scrutiny of skeptics. He then went on to transform the automotive industry with Tesla Motors, producing state-of-the-art, stylish, yet eco-friendly electric-powered vehicles. The innovative project was founded on Musk's vision of a world less dependent on oil.

Perhaps what separates Elon Musk from the average idealist is that he is an individual who not only dares to dream big, but also has the courage to venture into uncharted territory and attempt what has always been thought of as impossible. This fearlessness in following through on a vision, regardless of how absurd the vision may seem, is reflected in the creation of his space exploration company, SpaceX. Growing up with science fiction novels as his solace, Musk has held a bold dream for humanity: space colonization, his vision which he strongly believes could solve some of the problems humanity may be faced with in the current decades such as, but not limited to, world hunger.

Despite his awe inspiring achievements, Musk's journey so far has been far from smooth sailing.

Throughout his career as a tech genius and innovator, Musk has encountered his fair share of detractors, from skeptical business investors to opposing critics in various fields. Yet, he remained unfazed throughout his struggles and retained a firm belief in his vision of a better future for humankind. Through it all, Elon Musk has continued to defy what many believe to be impossible, pushing the boundaries of what oneself and humanity is capable of achieving.

There is a lot to be learned from the extraordinary life and career of Elon Musk. Those with wild ambitions and great visions will be curious to know how they can emulate Musk's success. As an old adage goes, we do not always have control over circumstances, but we can always exercise control over the way we react to things. In truth, it is not so much his genius, keen business sense and tireless hard work that made Elon Musk the success that he is, but rather how he faces up to hardship along the way. He often exhibits grit and determination, treating obstacles as challenges to overcome and learn from instead of letting himself become deterred.

In the chapters that follow, we will look more closely at some of the key concepts that have shaped Elon's attitude and beliefs which in turn have lead to his business and personal success. We will see that is not simply knowledge and education which is important, but rather a set of key principles that lead one to cultivate the mindset required for success in life and business. What's more adherence to moral principles can play a large part in ensuring one achieve long-term success, wealth and happiness. Who better than one of the greatest minds of our time to look to in order to learn these valuable lessons.

of inattention or otherwise, by any usage or abuse of any policies, processes, or directions contained within is the solitary and utter responsibility of the recipient reader. Under no circumstances will any legal responsibility or blame be held against the publisher for any reparation, damages, or monetary loss due to the information herein, either directly or indirectly.

Respective authors own all copyrights not held by the publisher.

The information herein is offered for informational purposes solely, and is universal as so. The presentation of the information is without contract or any type of guarantee assurance.

The trademarks that are used are without any consent, and the publication of the trademark is without permission or backing by the trademark owner. All trademarks and brands within this book are for clarifying purposes only and are the owned by the owners themselves, not affiliated with this document.

Table of contents

Chapter 1

The Importance Of Knowing What You Want And Why You Want It

"People work better when they know what the goal is and why."

Elon Musk

While many of us blindly go on with our days putting in endless hours of hard work, very few of us actually take the time to decide on what the end goal of all this hard work actually is. Truth is, as Elon Musk has said, knowing exactly what we want is vital to achieving long-term success and lasting fulfillment.

The trouble with not setting clear goals is that without them, we can end up "running around in circles" indefinitely. If we have no end goal in mind, we are simply leaving it to chance that our life will follow a favorable path and that we will reach a desirable destination. Without a mental map of where we are and where we want to get to, we it's very difficult (if not impossible) to make real progress toward meaningful goals. In addition, if we don't begin with the end in mind, we will oftentimes end up spending our entire lives putting in the work while gaining nothing of real importance in return for our efforts.

Let's take a simple scenario to illustrate the point: Let's imagine that we are a ship and life is an ocean. If we don't decide where we are headed, if we fail to set a bearing, the sea (in our analogy, "life") will take us wherever it pleases. We may get lucky and end up stumbling across an idyllic tropical island, replete with an abundance of food and all the necessities for a comfortable and enjoyable life.

Alternatively however, the sea may be less kind and smash our ship onto the rocks, leaving us floundering in treacherous seas. If we haven't made the decision to steer our ship on a course of our choosing, diligently checking and rechecking our course at regular intervals, we are effectively leaving our lives up to chance; if we're lucky things will end up going wonderfully, but the reality is there's a good chance we'll one day look back on our lives and think to ourselves, "How on earth did I end up here?!".

A second simple scenario to further illustrate the point: You're stranded on an island and need some form of shelter. If you simply cut wood day after day, will you be able to build a house? Even though you may be putting in the hard work, your actions alone will not magically create shelter. You must have an end vision and an understanding of why you are cutting the wood and how you will use it once it has been cut.

Similarly, if Elon Musk hadn't made the decision to have a hand in creating some of the most innovative technology of modern times, he wouldn't have achieved anything like the success that he has, and we wouldn't have (among other things) PayPal; the incredibly useful service that millions use to make financial transactions on a day to day basis!

Actions taken without an end goal in mind are an inefficient use of our energy as well as our resources. Setting a goal and envisioning a destination in our lives marks the first step on the path towards success. It's the only way we can achieve meaningful results. If you desire success, you've got to know what your definition of success is, how you plan to achieve it and exactly when you expect to reach your goal.

In addition, knowing what we want and why we want it gives us the drive which can propel us forward towards our goals. It will coax you to work hard and go the extra mile to achieve the success you desire in your life. We all have at some point in our lives worked like mad towards a goal that we set our mind to but then, over time as the excitement wanes, not all of us can keep on working with the same dedication or commitment. When we have a strong "why" for achieving a particular goal, be it in our business or our life, we will have a reason to put forth the extra effort; to fight that much harder to reach our goals. Having a strong vision of the reason as to why you want to achieve something can help you stay on track even when times get rough and your determination starts to waver.

Achieving success wasn't easy for Elon Musk. When he first started his own IT company , Zip2, he had to work for hours on end, live in the warehouse he used as his office and even go to locker rooms of local stadiums to take a shower! He dragged himself through all the tough times for two long years just to keep his fledgling company afloat. At times it must have been incredibly difficult for Elon to stay motivated and continue working towards his goals. Even the toughest of us can veer from our path when things get rough. Motivation and the initial excitement we feel at the start of a new endeavor are bound to fade over time, and this is why it's imperative that we have a clear vision and a strong enough reasons as to why we must achieve these goals.

Our work life is another area where we need to have a definite plan and a clear outcome in mind, as without one we may end up simply fulfilling others' goals rather that our own. Despite the fact that we may feel we are being "productive" during our working hours, in the long run, our hard work may simply be fulfilling someone else's end vision and may not be contributing to achieving our own personal goals. When we have a definite outcome in mind however, we're more likely to focus our energy, and the majority of our time and effort in the right direction.

Lastly, goals help us become the best we can be. Without an aim, without knowing what we want out of our life, we will oftentimes not be willing to step out of our comfort zones. But this tendency of not challenging ourselves and of not striving to go beyond what we find comfortable is a major hindrance in our personal growth. It obstructs us from discovering our true potential. With a goal in mind and well-laid out plans to achieve this goal in place, we will be forced to venture into new territory. We will be forced to learn new skills, polish our existing ones and as a result we will eventually grow to become better versions of ourselves.

Chapter 2

Embrace Change

"Some people don't like change, but you need to embrace change if the alternative is disaster."

Elon Musk

If we're honest, the fact is that very few of us like change. We love it when everything follows a regular routine, when things move at the same old pace and when our days go according to our regular routines and plans. It's the same for businesses as well; it would be wonderful if all of us could just stick to our "tried and tested" or "the same old" business strategies repeatedly to generate profits and reach the successes we desire. But like it or not, in today's fast moving environment, the worst decision that we can make in terms of our business, or indeed our life, is failing to embracing change.

Change is extremely important for any organization to succeed in the long run. If you don't evolve with your ever evolving customer base and fast changing market trends, you will soon lose your competitive edge, which can be the beginning of the end for many businesses. Simply put, failing to embrace change is a recipe for disaster. So why then do so many of us hesitate to embrace change?

The reason some of us feel so uncomfortable with change is because of the many uncertainties that accompany it. When we carry out a certain type of work and continue doing it for a long period of time, we get better at it, we get used to the workload, we become aware of what to expect and how to handle the tasks without any hassle. But all these certainties change when we venture into the unknown. We don't know what to expect anymore when we find ourselves in a new and unfamiliar situation. We may have to deal with curve balls that the new scenario might throw at us, and oftentimes doubt starts bubbling to the surface as we begin to wonder, "Am I going to be able to cope?". It makes sense therefore, that we would try to avoid change. However, as Elon Musk suggests, if we wish to be truly successful in business or in life, we've got to alter our perception of change and instead of looking at it as something negative, we must embrace it. We should try to see change as a chance for growth and self-improvement, and rather than fearing it, we should welcome it as a positive experience.

An example of Elon Musk embracing change? - he worked tirelessly for years behind his company Zip2 to make it a success. His strength and perseverance bore fruit in 1999. when AltaVista (the largest search engine at that time) bought Zip2 for $307 million and and $34 million in securities. If Musk so wished, he could have simply retired right then, enjoying the fruits of his success and spending the rest of his life sitting on a beach somewhere drinking cocktails. But he chose not to. He took a risk. Right after selling his company, Musk went onto pursue a completely different project, an electronic payment system, which later on emerged as PayPal, a service that millions of people from all over the world now use each and every day.

And he didn't stop there. Never wanting to become stagnant, he has pursued and achieved success in many more business ventures, one after another, after another. Right after the success of PayPal, he involved himself in space engineering and alternative energy sources. As a result, you can see where he has ended up today. Musk, is indeed a successful man but behind his success lies the fact that he was not afraid to embrace change. Truth is, even though change will be accompanied by uncertainties, it will bring new opportunities at the same time. And whether we like it or not, "change" is the only constant that any of us will ever find in our lives.

Chapter 3

Plan For The Worst To Prevent It From Happening

"If you want to grow a giant redwood, you need to make sure the seeds are ok, nurture the sapling, and work out what might potentially stop it from growing all the way along. Anything that breaks it at any point stops that growth."

Elon Musk

It's human nature to expect (or at least hope) that the course of all events will follow our initial plans when setting a goal. However, reality can be harsh and life seldom goes as planned. It's not possible for any of us to predict whether or not things will align with what we have in mind for the future. Hence, many of the most successful businessmen such as Musk, believe in the mantra, "Expect the best while planning for the worst".

You may have a goal planned out and things could be going full swing. You can see the pieces of the puzzle slowly forming the picture according to your plan, but then suddenly an unexpected obstacle appears out of nowhere that completely blocks the path you had laid out ahead. As you may already know from your own experiences, this is a very common occurrence both in life and in business, and most if not all successful people will have faced this type of adversity in their careers and their personal lives.

Elon Musk had to face an unexpected crisis during his time in Tesla Motors. Musk joined the project in 2004 and personally invested $70 million in the startup for the first electric car. The project was growing successfully, and even made it into the newspapers in 2006 all while attracting investments totaling up a staggering $100 million. But then in 2007, events started taking a turn for the worse when unexpected management failures caused a company crisis.

Planning for the worst even when things seem to be moving forward smoothly is a precaution that can, in the most extreme cases, really save your dreams from turning into nightmares. That's why it's imperative to, as Musk put it, "...work out what might potentially stop it from growing all the way along."

Whether your goals are related too your business or your personal life, it's wise to cover all the bases when in the very early stages of planning. This means thinking about all the scenarios that could potentially occur to scupper your plans, and doing your best to foresee any and all problems that could potentially arise further down the track.

Before starting out on a path, ask yourself the right questions. Ask yourself what could occur over the course of time that could disrupt the plan you've laid out. Ask yourself these questions regularly to ensure that you're keeping on the right path and are maintaining an awareness of the potential pitfalls. Answers (and possibly further questions) will arise, at which point you can begin taking measures to negate the issues before they occur. Create a solution for each scenario - what are the possible steps you could take to overcome each potential difficulty? Create contingency plans incase your initial plan fails. Formulate plan B beforehand so that during a time of crisis, you will be able to remain calm as you transition over to the alternative course of action.

The key here is to come up with a number of different plans that are ultimately able to lead you to the same end result. Therefore it's important that we take the time to think thoroughly and brainstorm in the early stages of any endeavor. Come up with alternative routes you could take to achieve your goal. Think about all the alternative actions that you could take for each step of your plan. While you may initially think that there's only one way of reaching your goal, the reality is there's always an alternative path. All you have to do to find it is to get a little creative and think outside of the box.

While some may say that planning for the worst is a form of negative thinking, the truth is that we cannot completely control every last factor that will lead to our ultimate success or failure. In fact, by taking steps to negate the chances of failure we are acting in a positive manner. The important thing to remember here is that we do not need to get too caught up on the possible difficulties we may face. We simply want to be aware of them, take steps to minimize the chances of them occurring, and then take action to move forward toward our desired goal. This approach will give us peace of mind, as we will have a safety net in place incase things start to go wrong.

Chapter 4

The Value Of Hard Work

"If there was a way that I could not eat,

so I could work more, I would not eat."

Elon Musk

All of the planning in the world won't help you achieve your goals unless you put in the required effort. Unfortunately, success is not something that can be achieved just by hoping for it. Even the best planning in the world won't be enough in and of itself. In order to be successful you have to have the strength to work hard towards your goal and to persevere when things get tough. This requires the right attitude and the ability to discipline yourself, as well as the self-control to prioritize your goals above nearly all else in life. A much as I myself would like to believe in shortcuts, the truth is, there is simply no alternative to hard work.

Ask any leading entrepreneur or business person about the secret behind their success, and you may be disappointed to hear that the "secret" is actually nothing but hour after hour of hard of arduous hard work. Sure, working smart is important and will help a great deal, as will planning effectively and some degree of natural ability. But no matter how well you implement these other criteria, nothing great will be achieved without the most important factor; plain old hard work.

Elon Musk himself used to work from early morning until late evening every single day during the time he was starting up Zip2. At that time he is said to have regularly worked for between 80 to 100 hours a week. In addition, he now manages to pull off the amazing feat of being the chief executive of both Tesla Motors and SpaceX, both at the same time! And let's not forget, he is also a father to 5 children. So, how does he manage his life and his work?

Simply put, Elon and others like him just work harder than the vast majority of people. While others are working 40 hours a week and relaxing on their down time, truly successful business people will have no problem putting in 80 to 100 hours per week if required. When anyone is putting that much time into achieving success, they will get things done faster than most, and are almost guaranteed to produce meaningful results which will eventually lead to the outcome they desire.

Something that would take a year for the average Joe to accomplish, a true hard worker could finish within a fraction of the time simply due to the number of hours they invest in moving toward their goal. They push themselves harder than most and are never satisfied with what they have done until it meets their own high standards.

A former employee at SpaceX shared that Musk's passion for his goals also influenced other employees in his company to work harder than they otherwise would. He would often push his employee's boundaries and force them to explore their higher potential.

In order to be successful in life, this is the type of work ethic that you need to cultivate. Strive to be the best version of yourself with each passing day and, quoting Elon Musk again, "Just work super hard!"

Chapter 5

Monitor Your Results And Question Your Actions

"I think that's the single best piece of advice: constantly think about how you could be doing things better and constantly question yourself."

Elon Musk

Even when we put forth the necessary effort and time for planning and taking action in order to advance towards our goals, few of us take the time to monitor the results of those actions and carefully track the progress we are making.

What we fail to realize is that, monitoring and evaluating our own actions plays a crucial role in determining how successful we will be in the long run. We need to constantly be checking in on how we are performing, both in our personal lives and in our businesses. We need to monitor whether or not our actions are bringing us the desired results, and we also need to question ourselves in order to discover other possible actions we could take which would help us improve the results we are getting. This process will require hard work and vigilance, but as I mentioned in the previous chapter, hard work is necessary if we have the desire to be the best versions of ourselves.

Take the example of Elon Musk, when his company Tesla Motors went spiraling downward in 2007. Rather than giving up on his venture he simply took stock, monitored the situation and evaluated the actions that led to the company's troubles, and then when he understood what had gone wrong he started doing things differently.

The first thing Musk did to fire all the employees in the company who were responsible for the development of the project being stalled. He realized that the company's financial resources were limited and that using those limited resources on these individuals was inefficient.

Next, Musk analyzed the business and evaluated how he could cut costs effectively without stripping the company of its core essentials. As a result, he reduced staff, negotiated with suppliers to lower prices, and took the step of closing a few offices. With these changes in effect, the company quickly began to turnaround again in 2008.

So, one of the key components of success is asking the right questions at the right times and understanding and observing how each of the actions that are being taken is affecting the outcome. It's crucial that we regularly ask ourselves if the actions we are taking are pushing us in the right direction and if the steps we have planned are likely to create the desired results. When our actions are not producing the outcomes we desire, we must then reassess, embrace change and do things differently.

Chapter 6

Take Risks

"When something is important enough, you do it even if the odds are not in your favor."

Elon Musk

Like it or not, taking risk goes hand in hand with entrepreneurship. When you have a desire to achieve greatness whether in your business life or your personal life, you simply can't shut your doors and avoid taking risks. Success is not something that comes to those who play within their comfort zones. In fact, the worst thing that any of us can do in terms of the development of our business or our growth as an individual is to fail to muster the courage to step out of our comfort zones.

I understand, feeling comfortable, having a steady paycheck and living with certainties , on the surface at least seems to be the ideal for many. But even if we ignore the fact that this lack of challenge rarely brings a true sense of satisfaction in the long run, there's also the question of just how sure can we be that this security will last into the future? Can you really be sure that your job will always be there to support you and the steady pay will continue to be there for you long-term? Reality is often harsh and the truth is, nothing in life is certain, especially factors as easily disrupted as the security of our jobs.

As it is in business, so it is in life. There is always the chance that circumstance will conspire to disrupt our lives, forcing us to leave our certainties behind and face the unknown. The only thing that has some semblance of security throughout our live is our own skills and talents (assuming we nurture them), and, if we make a constant effort to stay motivated, our drive and determination to succeed.

Therefore, if we really want our businesses to thrive or if we want to achieve great things in our lives, we have to take risks. This risk taking will come with no assurances of success, but to stagnate and to stay within our comfort zones will almost certainly lead to regression and failure to achieve our true potential. In the case of a new business, risk taking can come with many added burdens. For example you may have to take the plunge and use money from your own pocket to keep a fledgling company afloat. Sure, it's a risk, but assuming you believe it to be the best course of action it's likely a risk worth taking. When something is important to you, you're sometimes required to step outside your comfort zone and take a risk in order to achieve the desired outcome.

If Elon Musk had chosen to stay in his comfort zone rather than take a few risks, we wouldn't have seen the likes of Zip2, PayPal or Tesla Motors. Musk took his first notable risk was when he left his graduate school and rather than seeking a jobs in an established company, he decided to take the plunge and go ahead with his own IT startup, Zip2. At the time he was low on funds, and didn't have enough money to be able to afford both somewhere to live and an office space. Rather than be put of by this, he used his warehouse for both. Life wasn't comfortable for Musk, and on top of that, he was responsible for funding his fledgling company for the first two long years.

It was a risk that he decided to take against all odds as he had a clear vision of what he he wanted. Due to the fact he had this clear vision he was prepared to do whatever was necessary in order to make it a success. At that time the internet was experiencing rapid growth and Musk had no assurance that his company would end up being profitable. Despite the lack of certainty however, Musk followed his vision and, as is now evident for all to see, his risk and hard work more than paid off. Zip2 earned him a considerable sum of money when in 1999 AltaVista bought the company for $307 million.

While the majority of us view taking risk with negatively and trepidation, the reality is risks doorways to new opportunities for growth and success. On a biological level we are wired to fear risks. This fear kept us safe when we we're primitive humans as it still does in many situations today. If cavemen weren't afraid of saber-tooth tigers we wouldn't be here today, much like our fear of high places serves us in that it encourages us to be cautious when in a potentially life-threatening situation. However, we need to understand when our fears are helping us and when they are simply holding us back. We worry that taking risks is unwise and could lead to difficulties, but without taking the right risks at the right time, we will never achieve greatness.

Oftentimes, risk opens our eyes to unforeseen opportunities. Risks create the kind of environments that force our personal growth. Sure, taking risks is uncomfortable, but it's this discomfort which is critical for our success. This can be witnessed as so many companies often only reach their peak after going through crises which force them to develop in order to overcome these difficulties.

One such example that you can draw from in Elon Musk's life was his experience with Tesla Motors in 2008. At this time, Musk's company Tesla Motors was working on delivering its first electric car. However, due to unforeseen circumstances, Tesla had trouble in gathering the additional funds required to keep the company functioning.

When Musk realized his dream was slipping away from him, he decided to take a huge risk. He personally invested his last $20 million in cash to save the company. On top of this, he sacrificed his McLaren F1 to save the company from bankruptcy. He went as far as giving personal guarantees to customers in case the business failed. It was a huge gamble for Musk and it's unlikely that many entrepreneurs would have had the courage to take such personal financial risk.

However, Elon Musk showed bravery and belief in both his own abilities and his company. Judging by what has happened since we can clearly see that his risks paid off. Tesla Motors rose again with its incredible electric cars, and five years later Musk's stake in the company increased to $2.5 billon.

Even after so much success, Musk is repeatedly pushing himself out of his comfort zone once again. He has decided to sell company stock to repay money borrowed, with Musk himself planning to be one of the big buyers of these stocks as he intends to invest a huge $100 million in Tesla stocks! So, the moral of the story is, Musk's willingness to take risks is a major factor in the unbelievable success he has achieved.

If you are aiming to be successful, learn to embrace risk. Learn to challenge yourself and get used to uncomfortable situations. One of the best things that you can do for your career and for your life in general is to make it a habit to get out of your comfort zone. If you are a student, then perhaps forget about applying for jobs right out of college. If you are a businessman then stop limiting yourself within comfortable boundaries.

Start to see comfort as your enemy. If things in your life and career are going too smoothly, then it's time to shake things up a bit! It will feel daunting at first but challenging yourself to get out of your comfort zone will help you unleash your hidden talents. Why? Because when you are working in a particular field for a long time, you develop specific skill sets that you use on a regular basis. Since, you never need to stretch yourself to do anything different you tend to ignore the other strengths you possess, sometimes to such an extent that after years of non-use, you fail to realize that these strengths even exist. Shaking things up can help you find new areas of expertise. It can also help you learn new skills that you may not have even imagined you could possibly possess.

In addition to unlocking new or dormant talents, you may also find new interests while stepping into the unknown. How can you really know if you like something if you have never even tried it before?

There's only one way to find out: by taking the plunge. Musk may never have known how much he would love working in the fields of alternative energy and space technologies if he never taken certain risks earlier in his life.

Leaving your comfort zone is guaranteed to help you grow as a person. Stepping out of comfort and into the unknown will force you to learn, experience new things and speed up your personal growth. It will also make you capable of viewing things differently, giving you different perspectives and a fresh outlook on life. This expanded outlook and wider range of experiences will in turn give you an enhanced competitive edge, both in life and in business.

Uncomfortable situations teach us to be more adaptable when tackling challenging situations. When you start taking risks and in time are able to think outside of the box, the curve balls that life might throw you become that much easier to deal with.

Chapter 7

The Need For Patience and Persistence

"Patience is a virtue, and I'm learning patience. It's a tough lesson."

Elon Musk

We are all unique individuals with our own individual dreams and aspirations. The one thing that's common among the vast majority of us however is at least some amount of drive to succeed in one way or another. Yet, only a small number of us are ever likely to make our dreams a reality. So the question is, what exactly are the successful among us doing differently?

If I have learned anything from Elon Musk's life, it's the fact that success cannot be achieved without "the three P's": Patience, Persistence and Perseverance. These three P's are essential if you want to achieve any meaningful successful in life, for nothing worth having comes easy or instantly. You can't expect to work for a day and suddenly become a millionaire.

Let's look at it from a different angle; when you plant a sapling, it eventually grows into a tree assuming that you water and nurture it regularly. However can you actually see it growing as you are looking at it? Do you really see any changes on a daily basis? Of course not, and it's the same with business and with your life. You work on whatever it is that you want to achieve, you nurture it with your foresight and hard work, but you can't usually see or feel any dramatic changes on a day to day basis. This is because everything takes time to grow and develop, just like a sapling growing into a tree.

You may not be able to see the effect your work is having immediately, but that doesn't mean that you are not advancing. You have to realize that the best things in life are worth working for, and the vast majority of them will also require patience and persistence. Success does not come over night and often takes years to achieve.

You could point to all the "overnight success stories" found on the Internet as proof that what I'm saying isn't always true. Well, the internet these days is full of overnight success stories, but those stories are "overnight successes" because they don't mention all the years it took to lay the foundation which allowed the success to occur. They only focus on the fruit, not the years of labour involved in growing and caring for the tree that bore it.

If you read Elon Musk's biography, you will find that it took him years and years of hard work to reach the point where he is today. As mentioned earlier, when he started his first IT Company, he had to work like a maniac for 2 long years before he got his first real taste of success. If Musk would have focused on the fact he was not getting any immediate results despite the hard work he was putting in, he may have just dropped his idea and moved on to the next. But because he stuck with it and saw his idea through, the company was a major success and the eventual sale of the company made Musk a very wealthy man. Patience is one of the keys to success. You have got to believe that your hard work will pay off eventually and stick with your dream until you reach your desired outcome. You will only lose if you give in too early.

The other key is persistence. Musk continued with his project of creating electric cars at Tesla motors even when things turned sour. He didn't give up because he believed in his dream and he believed that if he persistently worked towards it, one day his vision would materialize and become a reality. He personally invested millions of dollars in Tesla and had to be patient while working persistently for 5 long years before he could achieve the success he had been striving for.

As Musk says "Patience is a virtue, and I'm learning patience. It's a tough lesson". Being patient and persistent can be difficult at times, but when you have your heart set on something, you need to have patience and the commitment to follow through in order to achieve your end goal.

You might be surprised to know that Elon Musk invested $10 million in SolarCity Corporation in 2003 because the company philosophy coincided with his principles. The company's concept was one of being cost-effective and eco-friendly. However, when Elon invested the funds, the company was yet to mature to the peak of its success. Even though critics said SolarCity didn't possess an effective business model, in 2012 the company stock prices increased considerably. As of now, the total market cap is estimated to be around $5.53 billion with Musk owning 25% of the company, and once again Musk proved to the world that persistence and patience really does pay off in the long run.

Even in the case of SpaceX, another of Musk's companies which is involved in space exploration technologies, Musk has displayed his perseverant nature. From 2006 to 2008, SpaceX was doing everything it could to launch its space craft, but unfortunately, the first three attempts failed and millions of dollars of investment went down the drain. If Musk had of chosen to give up and not persevere then perhaps SpaceX would no longer be here today. Musk was wise to keep on fighting to achieve his goal despite the hardships. He gathered enough financial support to allow further flight attempts and then finally on the 28th of September 2008, SpaceX successfully launched its Falcon 1 rocket into the earth's orbit.

Elon once again showed us all that with perseverance you can achieve whatever you set your mind on. All you have to do to reach your goal, is keep on fighting against all the odds until you finally arrive.

As of now, Elon is working on his concept of a fifth mode of transport called the Hyperloop. Undoubtedly, Elon will show the same patience, persistence and perseverance that have lead to him being successful so many times before.

Take a lesson from Elon; focus on the three P's: Patience, Persistence and Perseverance. Remember to be patient both in terms of the achievement of goals related to your work   life and in terms the achievement of any personal goals you may have. Fully commit yourself to whatever it is you are doing, and when you face challenges, make sure you put up a good fight and don't give up. Whats more, learn to enjoy the challenges you face and remember that they are aiding your personal growth and development as you move towards your ideal vision.

Chapter 8

Noteworthy & Inspirational Quotes

On his favorite book when he was a teen, "The Hitchhiker's Guide to the Galaxy": It taught me that the tough thing is figuring out what questions to ask, but that once you do that, the rest is really easy."

– Elon Musk

"I just want to retire before I go senile because if I don't retire before I go senile, then I'll do more damage than good at that point."

– Elon Musk

"I would like to die on Mars. Just not on impact."

– Elon Musk

On his favorite book when he was a teen, "The Hitchhiker's Guide to the Galaxy": It taught me that the tough thing is figuring out what questions to ask, but that once you do that, the rest is really easy."

– Elon Musk

"Don't be afraid of new arenas."

– Elon Musk

"I just want to retire before I go senile because if I don't retire before I go senile, then I'll do more damage than good at that point."

– Elon Musk

"I could either watch it happen or be a part of it."

– Elon Musk

"Failure is an option here. If things are not failing, you are not innovating enough."

– Elon Musk

"If something is important enough, even if the odds are against you, you should still do it."

– Elon Musk

"Going from PayPal, I thought: 'Well, what are some of the other problems that are likely to most affect the future of humanity?' Not from the perspective, 'What's the best way to make money?"

– Elon Musk

"(Physics is) a good framework for thinking. ... Boil things down to their fundamental truths and reason up from there."

– Elon Musk

"Brand is just a perception, and perception will match reality over time. Sometimes it will be ahead, other times it will be behind. But brand is simply a collective impression some have about a product."

– Elon Musk

"The first step is to establish that something is possible; then probability will occur."

– Elon Musk

"You want to be extra rigorous about making the best possible thing you can. Find everything that's wrong with it and fix it. Seek negative feedback, particularly from friends."

– Elon Musk

"It's OK to have your eggs in one basket as long as you control what happens to that basket."

– Elon Musk

"Persistence is very important. You should not give up unless you are forced to give up."

– Elon Musk

"Starting and growing a business is as much about the innovation, drive and determination of the people who do it as it is about the product they sell."

– Elon Musk

"Failure is an option here. If things are not failing, you are not innovating enough."

– Elon Musk

"If something is important enough, even if the odds are against you, you should still do it."

– Elon Musk

"Going from PayPal, I thought: 'Well, what are some of the other problems that are likely to most affect the future of humanity?' Not from the perspective, 'What's the best way to make money?"

– Elon Musk

"(Physics is) a good framework for thinking. ... Boil things down to their fundamental truths and reason up from there."

– Elon Musk

"Brand is just a perception, and perception will match reality over time. Sometimes it will be ahead, other times it will be behind. But brand is simply a collective impression some have about a product."

– Elon Musk

"You want to have a future where you're expecting things to be better, not one where you're expecting things to be worse."

– Elon Musk

"It is a mistake to hire huge numbers of people to get a complicated job done. Numbers will never compensate for talent in getting the right answer (two people who don't know something are no better than one), will tend to slow down progress, and will make the task incredibly expensive."

– Elon Musk

"You have to be pretty driven to make it happen. Otherwise, you will just make yourself miserable."

– Elon Musk

"Work like hell. I mean you just have to put in 80 to 100 hour weeks every week. [This] improves the odds of success. If other people are putting in 40 hour work weeks and you're putting in 100 hour work weeks, then even if you're doing the same thing you know that... you will achieve in 4 months what it takes them a year to achieve."

– Elon Musk

"If you go back a few hundred years, what we take for granted today would seem like magic – being able to talk to people over long distances, to transmit images, flying, accessing vast amounts of data like an oracle. These are all things that would have been considered magic a few hundred years ago."

– Elon Musk

"Being an Entrepreneur is like eating glass and staring into the abyss of death"

– Elon Musk

"When I was in college, I wanted to be involved in things that would change the world. Now I am."

– Elon Musk

"Life is too short for long-term grudges."

– Elon Musk

"I think it's very important to have a feedback loop, where you're constantly thinking about what you've done and how you could be doing it better. I think that's the single best piece of advice: constantly think about how you could be doing things better and questioning yourself."

– Elon Musk

"Being an Entrepreneur is like eating glass and staring into the abyss of death"

– Elon Musk

"I think it's very important to have a feedback loop, where you're constantly thinking about what you've done and how you could be doing it better. I think that's the single best piece of advice: constantly think about how you could be doing things better and questioning yourself."

– Elon Musk

"I would like to die on Mars. Just not on impact."

– Elon Musk

On his favorite book when he was a teen, "The Hitchhiker's Guide to the Galaxy": It taught me that the tough thing is figuring out what questions to ask, but that once you do that, the rest is really easy."

– Elon Musk

"I just want to retire before I go senile because if I don't retire before I go senile, then I'll do more damage than good at that point."

– Elon Musk

"People work better when they know what the goal is and why. It is important that people look forward to coming to work in the morning and enjoy working."

– Elon Musk

"My biggest mistake is probably weighing too much on someone's talent and not someone's personality. I think it matters whether someone has a good heart."

– Elon Musk

"[As a child] I would just question things…"

– Elon Musk

"I think it is possible for ordinary people to choose to
be extraordinary."

– Elon Musk

"Let's think beyond the normal stuff and have an environment where that sort of thinking is encouraged and rewarded and where it's okay to fail as well. Because when you try new things, you try this idea, that idea… well a large number of them are not gonna work, and that has to be okay. If every time somebody comes up with an idea it has to be successful, you're not gonna get people coming up with ideas."

– Elon Musk

"I came to the conclusion that we should aspire to increase the scope and scale of human consciousness in order to better understand what questions to ask. Really, the only thing that makes sense is to strive for greater collective enlightenment."

– Elon Musk

"Patience is a virtue, and I'm learning patience. It's a tough lesson."

– Elon Musk

"When I was in college, I wanted to be involved in things that would change the world. Now I am."

– Elon Musk

"If you're trying to create a company, it's like baking a cake. You have to have all the ingredients in the right proportion."

– Elon Musk

"I think it's very important to have a feedback loop, where you're constantly thinking about what you've done and how you could be doing it better. I think that's the single best piece of advice: constantly think about how you could be doing things better and questioning yourself."

– Elon Musk

"I wouldn't say I have a lack of fear. In fact, I'd like my fear emotion to be less because it's very distracting and fries my nervous system."

– Elon Musk

"My motivation for all my companies has been to be involved in something that I thought would have a significant impact on the world."

– Elon Musk

"If something's important enough, you should try. Even if you – the probable outcome is failure."

– Elon Musk

"You shouldn't do things differently just because they're different. They need to be... better."

– Elon Musk

"I think life on Earth must be about more than just solving problems. It's got to be something inspiring, even if it is vicarious."

– Elon Musk

"The idea of lying on a beach as my main thing just sounds like the worst. It sounds horrible to me. I would go bonkers. I would have to be on serious drugs. I'd be super-duper bored. I like high intensity."

– Elon Musk

'I don't know whether our technology level will keep going, or subside. For the first time in four and half billion years, the technology level is at a point where we can extend life to another planet; make life multi-planetary. I think it's too easy to take for granted that it's going to stay above that level, and if it doesn't, if it falls below that, will it return? Who knows. The sun is gradually expanding and in about roughly 500 million years -- maybe a billion years at the outside -- the oceans will boil, and there will be no meaningful life on Earth. I mean there might be like some chemotrophs or ultra-high temperature bacteria or something, but nothing that can make a spaceship. And you might think 'that's a 500 million year time frame', but it's only a 10% increase in the lifespan of Earth. So "if humanity had taken an extra 10% longer to get here, it wouldn't have gotten here at all."

– Elon Musk

<u>Conclusion</u>

Elon Musk could easily be called a modern day renaissance man. His abilities seem unlimited and he is unquestionably a supremely driven individual who has already achieved some truly outstanding feats. Not only that, but he is still a relatively young man and with his seemingly insatiable drive and ambition it seems almost inevitable that he will achieve much more during the remainder of his life.

The truth is, very few of us are likely to have such lofty ambitions as Musk. Despite this we can however still learn a great deal from him in regard to what it takes to be successful, both in business and in life. I hope the ideas presented in this book have given you food for thought and that you will apply some of the principles exhibited by Musk in order to push yourself

forward toward achieving your own goals.

FREE BONUS!: Preview Of

"Warren Buffett - The

Business & Life Lessons Of

An Investment Genius,

Magnate & Philanthropist"!

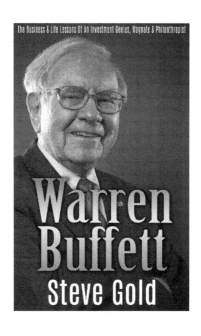

If you enjoyed this book, I have a little bonus for you; a preview of one of my other books "Warren Buffett - The Business & Life Lessons Of An Investment Genius, Magnate & Philanthropist". In this book, I take a closer look at exactly who Warren Buffett is as well as examining the truly extraordinary accomplishments he has managed to achieve in his life thus far. In the book I dig deeper into 7 of the major principles that have helped Buffett achieve such unbelievable success. Enjoy the free sample, and feel free to click on the purchase link below if you would like to learn more about this truly incredible individual!

<u>Introduction</u>

It may be a bold statement, but I believe that no one in the world of investment who's alive today understands success, wealth and, perhaps even happiness, the way that Warren Buffet does. Not only does the so-called "Sage of Omaha" know how to generate an immense fortune, he also has a solid comprehension of how finite and impermanent money actually is. He may have made a name for himself as an investment strategist, but Buffet often speaks of how loose and overrated the link between wealth and quality of life can be. He would even go as far as to stress – somewhat paradoxically – that the more money one has, the less free and unhappy one is likely to become.

Indeed, it can almost seem at times that despite his influential career in finance, Buffett does not place great importance on money and material possessions. His net worth may be up in the billions, but he lives in the least billionaire-like fashion. Buffett, who's the antithesis of the typical image of a wealthy business magnate, owns a considerably modest amount of tangible assets compared to his nine-figure net worth peers, and he appears to be disinterested in the extravagant lifestyle of the rich and famous. He embraces the simplicity of daily life, reminding himself from the onset of his career that there are no greater assets one can possess than good health, as well as remembering that the key to happiness lies in the priceless bonds one creates with friends and family.

His impartiality to wealth could not be more evident than in his numerous philanthropic efforts, which includes record-breaking donations amounting to more than half of his accumulated wealth over time.

Regardless of where one stands in life and whatever one's aspirations are, plenty can be learned by examining the core values that made Warren Buffett one of the most successful and wealthy individuals in the world.

In the chapters that follow, you will see that business and personal success is not so much a result of strategic investment decisions, but rather it results from cultivating a number of personality traits essential for navigating the world of commerce.

Additionally, as Buffett has continuously demonstrated, good character and adherence to moral principles goes a long way in ensuring long-term success, wealth and happiness.

Warren Buffet has made great contributions to the world in the form of a long-standing investment track-record along with his enormously generous philanthropic endeavors. As a business and investment magnate, Buffett's approach to growing and managing wealth contains a certain humility that is so rarely given attention in a field that is predominantly about strategies and figures. Drawing from his own life experiences, Buffett acknowledges the human element that is often overlooked when it comes to accumulating and maintaining wealth. His philosophy and principles are simple, yet so powerful that they go beyond investment portfolios and apply to practically every aspect of our lives.

Buffett's extensive career achievements, however, can never measure up to the impressive life he has led. Living by his beliefs and principles, he proves that with patience, perseverance, diligence and hard work, one can build a financially stable and fulfilling life. Most importantly, he has exemplifies that a quality life is one which is lived with generosity, integrity and modesty.

Chapter 1

Plan For The Future

"Someone's sitting in the shade today because someone planted a tree a long time ago."

Warren Buffett

The path to financial and personal success is not lined with gold but with golden values.

Keeping your path straight, free from distractions or temptations, is the best vision anybody can take while planning their financial future. Investment strategists such as Warren Buffett suggest instilling in yourself from a young age the ability to stick with your plan following concrete steps to get to where you want to be.

Buffett had a vision from when he was a child that he would be rich by investing his money in himself instead of giving away his hard earned money to somebody else. That vision started when he was a young boy in Washington, D.C., where his father served four terms in the U.S. House of Representatives after moving the family from Omaha, Neb. His father was originally a stockbroker and

Warren learned the trade of investing by being close to his father. As a teenager in D.C., Buffett invested in placing pinball machines in barbershops. He took the money from those pinball machines and invested in more machines.

He was fortunate from the beginning to have a father who stressed the importance of making sound financial decisions to improve his future. Every bit of his money was important to his development in becoming the second wealthiest person in America, behind business magnate Bill Gates.

Buffett, who was born on Aug. 30, 1930, stresses to young people today to grasp what they have and build on it before giving it away to credit card companies.

He warns against spending sprees and living outlandishly. His message: Everything has a price and what you spend today will affect your savings for tomorrow, not only for yourself but for your children and grandchildren.

"Money doesn't create man, but it is the man who created money," Buffett said in a recent interview with CNBC.

Money does not define Buffett although he is worth billions. He has maintained his humble values from his modest upbringing in Omaha. He continues to live in the same home in Omaha that he bought in 1958 for $31,500. The 6,000-square foot home in the Dundee-Happy Hollow Historic is valued today at

$250,000, still a modest price for the mega-billionaire who is nicknamed the "Oracle of Omaha".

It is the only house Buffett owns, which is another rarity for a billionaire who has more personal wealth than some third-world countries. He once also owned real estate in Laguna Beach, Calif., but sold that property in 2005 for $5.45 million, a profit of more than $4 million from when he purchased it in 1993 as a vacation spot for him and his wife. Even when he tried to live lavishly, he made a profit from it, although this was an isolated case where he strayed from his basic principles.

Buffett always had a clear vision of his future since his childhood. He became an investor when he was 11. In his high school yearbook, he described himself as a "future stockbroker" although he was well on his way. From the start, he had the confidence to achieve his goals because he knew his path would be free of distractions or temptations. He was never consumed by excess to a fault.

"I don't think standard of living equates with cost of living beyond a certain point," Buffett said about his modest home during a 2014 shareholder meeting for Berkshire Hathaway, an American multinational conglomerate holding company that he owns. "Good housing, good health, good food, good transport. There's a point you start getting inverse correlation between wealth and quality of life. My life couldn't be happier. In fact, it'd be worse if I had six or eight houses. So, I have everything I need to have, and I don't need any more because it doesn't make a difference after a point."

Buffett is on record saying that having more wealth actually reduces the quality of life. In his opinion, the quality of life is based on basic needs. That includes having good health, adequate housing, nourishment and transportation. Not all who are afforded these needs are content or satisfied. People crave bigger homes, souped-up cars and meals at expensive restaurants. Many of us believe happiness comes from having an extravagant lifestyle.

Buffett's clear vision of his future from the time he was raised in Omaha and Washington, D.C., has allowed him to become wealthier than even the greediest person can imagine. The invaluable plans from when Buffett was young that created his happy existence involved taking an inventory of his life, embracing the simplicity of his life and never straying from his core values.

When taking an inventory of his life during his formative years at the University of Nebraska and Columbia Business School, Buffett realized his greatest asset aside from his health was his association with his significant other, family and long-standing friends. His inherent assets – his personality, humor and education -- all played a part in his fruitful association with others. They carry no price tag. Those assets define him more than money ever will.

Buffett's simple pleasures of life include keeping to himself, reading a book without interruption. His idea of a pleasurable evening since his high school years is not being out on the town but instead staying home to watch television and enjoy a hot cup of tea. Buffett believes that taking every opportunity to embrace your simple pleasures is the most valuable move you can make for your future.

Throughout the years, Buffett has stayed true to his core principles and values. He never takes a chance with his investments. He sticks with investing in the sectors he believes will produce the most profit. Maintaining a clear vision of the values needed to reach prosperity has allowed Buffett to stay atop the business world, never wavering.

Check out the rest of "Warren Buffett - The Business & Life Lessons Of An Investment Genius, Magnate & Philanthropist" on Amazon.

Check Out My Other Books!

Elon Musk - The Biography Of A Modern Day

Renaissance ManElon Musk - The Business & Life Lessons Of A Modern Day Renaissance Man

Warren Buffett - The Business And Life Lessons Of An Investment Genius, Magnate And Philanthropist

Steve Jobs - The Biography & Lessons Of The Mastermind Behind Apple

Management - Achieve Management Excellence & World Class Leadership Skills In 7 Simple Steps

Sales - Easily Sell Anything To Anyone & Achieve Sales Excellence In 7 Simple Steps

Arduino - Getting Started With Arduino: The Ultimate Beginner's Guide

(If the links do not work, for whatever reason, you can simply search for these titles on the Amazon to find them. All books available as ebooks or printed books)

Printed in Great Britain
by Amazon